TRANSFORMERS

by Sue Bradford Edwards

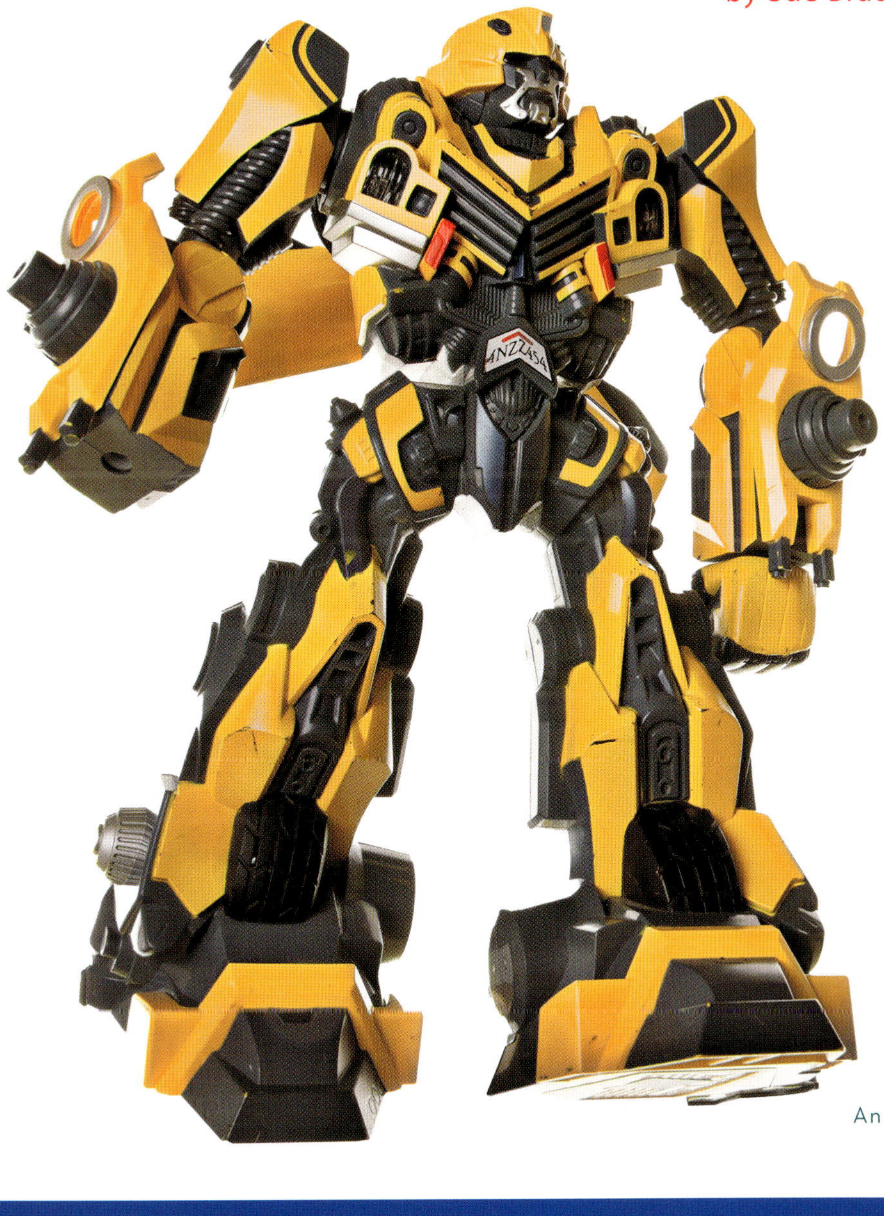

Early Encyclopedias

An Imprint of Abdo Reference

abdobooks.com

abdobooks.com

Published by Abdo Reference, a division of ABDO, PO Box 398166, Minneapolis, Minnesota 55439.

Printed in China.
052025
092025

Editor: Laura Stickney
Series Designers: Candice Keimig, Joshua Olson
Production Designer: Pat Maloney

Library of Congress Control Number: 2024949358

Publisher's Cataloging-in-Publication Data

Names: Edwards, Sue Bradford, author.
Title: Transformers / by Sue Bradford Edwards
Description: Minneapolis, Minnesota: Abdo Reference, 2026 | Series: Early toy encyclopedias | Includes online resources and index.
Identifiers: ISBN 9781098297596 (lib. bdg.) | ISBN 9798384930112 (ebook)
Subjects: LCSH: Transformers (Fictitious characters)--Juvenile literature. | Motion pictures--Juvenile literature. | Television programs--Juvenile literature. | Toys--Juvenile literature. | Collectibles--Juvenile literature. | Reference materials--Juvenile literature. | Encyclopedias and dictionaries--Juvenile literature.
Classification: DDC 791.4375--dc23

CONTENTS

One slogan for Transformers is "More than meets the eye."

Iconic Toys

Transformers are giant robots. They come from the planet Cybertron. These toys have been popular with US fans since 1984. But Transformers began in Japan.

Microman

Takara is a Japanese toy company. It created Microman toys. These came out in Japan.

They were released in 1974. Each Microman was 3.75 inches (9.5 cm) tall. The action figures had clear bodies. They could be put into poses.

Diaclone

In 1980, Takara introduced another toy line. Diaclone were robots. They turned into cars. Microman and Diaclone toys had the same connectors. Kids could take the toys apart. They could build their own robots.

Japanese toy makers made many futuristic robot toys in the 1960s and 1970s.

The Micronauts line featured heroes and villains. One 1977 figure was the villain Baron Karza, who had magnetic limbs.

Microman Cyborgs

Ads said Micromans were cyborgs. They came from Micro Earth. On Earth, the cyborgs disguised themselves as toys.

Micronauts

Mego is a toy company. In 1976, it started selling Micronauts. These were sold in the United States. Many were like Micromans. But some were new figures.

Hasbro

Hasbro is a US toy company. In 1983, it bought the right to sell Microman, Micronaut, and Diaclone toys. It renamed them Transformers. Hasbro made the toys bigger. But they still transformed.

Early Hasbro Transformers were packaged in their vehicle forms. The box included pictures that showed what the toys looked like in robot form.

TV Series

Hasbro made a TV series. It was called *Transformers*. It appeared on TV in 1984. The cartoon taught kids about the toys. Soon, many kids had favorite Transformers.

The Story

In *Transformers*, two groups leave Cybertron. They are the Autobots and Decepticons. They seek

The cartoon *Transformers* featured original characters. It also introduced new characters, such as Silverbolt, that were later made into toys.

Optimus Prime was a recurring character in *Transformers*. The first Optimus Prime toy turned into a Freightliner FLA 8664 truck and trailer.

an energy source. It is called Energon. The robots crash on Earth. They wake up in 1984. The Decepticons want to take over Earth. The Autobots protect the planet.

Cartoons and Movies

In two years, the cartoon had become popular. Its creators made a movie. It was *The Transformers: The Movie*. It came out in 1986. It is animated.

Transformers Today

Today, many Transformers are sold. The smallest fits in one hand. Others are large. One is Fortress Maximus. It is 22 inches (56 cm) tall. It is 11 pounds (5 kg).

Fortress Maximus, *right*, is the largest figure from the G1 line. The toy was first released in 1987.

The Transformers: The Movie featured the tagline "Beyond good. Beyond evil. Beyond your wildest imagination."

Games and Books

There are many ways to enjoy Transformers. Fans can read books. They can play Transformers games. Some games are for phones. Others are for computers and consoles. Some are crossovers.

In 2014, the crossover game *Angry Birds Transformers* was released. It featured *Angry Birds* characters in robot armor and helmets.

Today, Hasbro offers Transformers toys for kids of all ages. Some are designed for preschoolers, while others are for teens.

Many Lines

Transformers have been reimagined many times. Sometimes they turn into beasts. In other toy lines, they become machines. Over time, new Transformers have been added. Their story has grown. They continue to gain fans.

Standing Out

In 1984, several companies sold robot toys. Hasbro wanted people to recognize its toys. In 1985, Hasbro added a rubsign to the toys. This was a sticker. It got warm when rubbed. This made a sign appear.

The first Transformer toys with rubsigns were called Mini-spies.

Exciting Episodes

In each *Transformers* episode, Autobots fight Decepticons. Fans meet characters. These include Starscream and Soundwave. Bumblebee and Jazz also appear. The series ended in 1987.

Frank Welker

One actor, Frank Welker, has voiced many Decepticons. He played Megatron, Soundwave, and Skywarp. He also voiced Rumble, Frenzy, and Ravage.

First Figures

There were originally 28 Transformers. Fans could turn Hound into a jeep. Wheeljack became a race car. The toys sold well. Later, Takara renamed the toys sold in Japan. It called them Transformers.

Jazz was one of the original Transformer figures. He turned into a car with stripes and the number 4 printed on it.

Optimus Prime

Optimus Prime leads the Autobots. He is a popular Transformer. One Optimus Prime was from the Generation 1 (G1) line. He turned into a truck. The truck's trailer opened into a combat deck.

The G1 Optimus Prime figure came with accessories such as a black rifle. In robot form, the cab of a truck formed Optimus Prime's chest.

Arcee

Arcee is a strong warrior. She is good at hand-to-hand fighting. No G1 Arcee figures were made. But she was a popular character on the show. Later, many Arcee figures were made.

Many Arcee figures are pink and white. They include a backpack and round helmet.

Bumblebee

In Japan, Bumblebee is called Bumble.

Bumblebee is a yellow-and-black robot. He fights for those who cannot defend themselves. He befriends humans. The G1 Bumblebee turned into a Volkswagen Beetle.

Many different Bumblebee toys have been released over the years. One is the 2007 Cyber Stompin' Bumblebee.

Hot Rod

Hot Rod dives into battle without thinking. He turns into a sports car. Later, Hot Rod becomes the Autobots' leader. He is called Rodimus Prime. He turns into a truck.

Ironhide

Ironhide is red and boxy. He has a temper. He helps Optimus Prime. He has a rare gun. It can create liquids. Then it fires the liquid.

Jazz

Jazz is interested in human cultures. He is a good student. He loves music. The G1 Jazz transforms into a Porsche 935. He blasts enemies with sound and light.

The 1986 Hot Rod figure was red, yellow, and orange. It featured a flame pattern.

In some toy lines and cartoons, Ironhide is gray. Someone wore a costume of this character at the 2013 Dublin Comic Con in Ireland.

Metroplex

Metroplex is big and strong. His G1 figure turns into a base. The base looks like a city. He also turns into an aircraft carrier.

Hasbro released the Generations Titan Class Metroplex. This figure stood more than 2 feet (0.6 m) tall.

Omega Supreme

Omega Supreme protects Crystal City. This is on Cybertron. Omega Supreme turns into a transport ship. He also turns into a rocket base.

FUN FACT!

In 2023, a boxed Omega Supreme G1 figure was worth about $500.

Ratchet

Ratchet is a soldier and medic. He fights. But he is also a scientist. He fixes other Autobots. Ratchet changes into an ambulance.

Many Omega Supreme figures have a giant claw hand.

Wheeljack

Wheeljack turns into a race car. But he can also fly. He has rockets in his arms. He is a scientist too. Sometimes he builds new Autobots. He created the Dinobots.

FUN FACT!

Wheeljack is the first Transformer to appear in the cartoon.

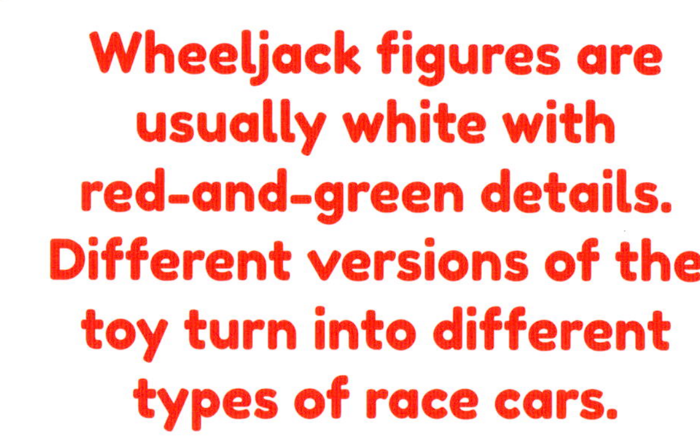

Wheeljack figures are usually white with red-and-green details. Different versions of the toy turn into different types of race cars.

Grimlock

Grimlock leads the Dinobots. His dinosaur form is a T. rex. He has strong jaws. He is hard to beat. This makes Grimlock an asset in battle.

The 2014 Stomp & Chomp Grimlock could transform from a robot to a dinosaur in one step. Kids pulled a handle to make the toy transform.

Megatron

Megatron leads the Decepticons. He is evil and destructive. But he thinks he is good. Megatron originally changed into a laser pistol. In this form, another robot carried him.

FUN FACT!

At first, Hasbro didn't like Megatron's name. The company thought it was too scary.

Blitzwing

Blitzwing is a Decepticon. He turns into a fighter jet. He also becomes a tank. Each form has weapons. One is a superheater cannon. Another can freeze enemies.

The G1 Megatron was silver and had a black cannon mounted on its arm.

Most Blitzwing figures are purple. Some versions include a spring-loaded cannon that fires missiles.

Cyclonus

Cyclonus is powerful and smart. But he is coldhearted. He won't back down. He is also loyal. He won't try to overthrow Megatron. He turns into a jet.

In 2016, a special-edition Cyclonus figure was released. It featured translucent purple plastic.

Ravage

Ravage has no vehicle form. Instead, he turns into a panther. In this form, he cannot be seen. He scouts enemy areas. Ravage changes into a cassette too. In this form, he is stored in Soundwave's chest.

Later versions of Ravage transformed into a black car.

Most Starscream figures feature red and blue colors.

Starscream

Starscream is Megatron's second-in-command. He wants to be in charge. Sometimes he tries to take over. Megatron does not trust him. Starscream turns into a fighter jet.

Trypticon

Trypticon transforms into a city. He has landing and repair bays. He changes into a reptile too. Trypticon also turns into a battle station. It has laser cannons and blasters.

Several mini Transformers serve as parts of the G1 Trypticon figure. A purple robot is his chest plate.

Soundwave

Soundwave is a Decepticon. He sends messages. His chest is a cassette recorder. He carries minions in it. He sends them to collect information. Soundwave has a computerized voice.

Voicing Soundwave

Frank Welker voiced Soundwave. His voice was changed to sound computerized. By mistake, his voice was unchanged in two episodes.

The G1 Soundwave figure came packaged in cassette recorder form. The toy included the cassette Buzzsaw, *top left*.

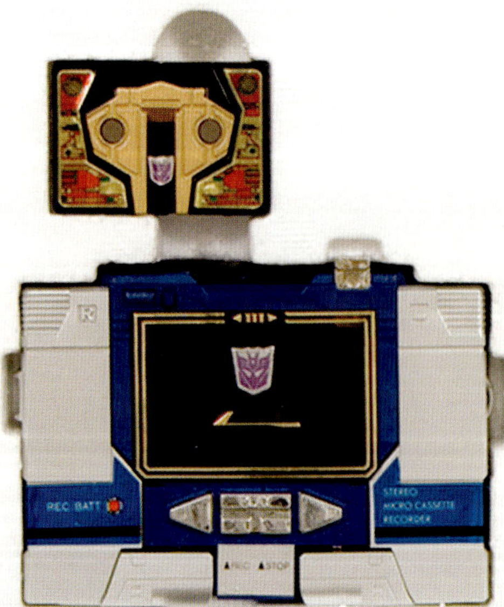

Devastator is made up of pieces of construction vehicles, including a dump truck, cement mixer, and crane.

Laserbeak

Laserbeak is one of Soundwave's cassettes. He turns into a bird-like creature. Laserbeak is good at finding hiding spots. He spies on Autobots.

Devastator

Six Decepticons are Constructicons. They combine to form Devastator. He is purple and green. He carries a solar energy rifle. His armor is bulletproof. It protects him from radiation.

First Video Game

The first Transformers video game came out in 1986. It was *The Transformers*. It is for home computers. Players search a city. To win, they must find parts of an Energon cube.

In early Transformers video games and cartoons, Energon cubes were pink. Some Transformers toys came with Energon cubes.

Mystery of Convoy

Some games were released only in Japan. One was *Transformers: Mystery of Convoy.* Takara published it in 1986. Fans play as Ultra Magnus. They must find who is behind Optimus Prime's death.

Transformers: Mystery of Convoy **was designed for the Nintendo Famicom gaming system.**

Marvel Comics

Marvel published the first Transformers comics. The company planned a series. It is about Transformers arriving on Earth. The books were popular. Marvel published more comics. The series ran from 1984 to 1991.

One 1985 Transformers comic features a human character called Brick Springstern. He is based on the singer Bruce Springsteen.

Marvel published Transformers Annuals in the 1980s and 1990s. These books included comics, games, character spotlights, and more.

Marvel Books

Marvel published other books. *Battle for Earth* came out in 1985. It is for young readers. Two coloring books were released too. *Invasion of the Decepticon Camp* came out in 1986. So did *The Lost Treasure of Cybertron*.

Find Your Fate

Many Transformers books were released. Ballantine Books published nine. They were Find Your Fate books. They came out in 1985 and 1986. Readers choose what characters do next. Each book has several endings. The first book was *Dinobots Strike Back*. The second was *Battle Drive*.

The first Ballantine Find Your Fate book featured the character Bombshell, who could transform into a bug.

Books and Cassettes

Ladybird Books created more Transformers books. Each book had an audio cassette. Actors read the story. The audio included music. It had sound effects. Ten books were released. They came out between 1985 and 1988.

In 1986, Ladybird Books published stories that featured Ultra Magnus. Hasbro released a G1 figure of the Transformer that same year.

Hot Rod is one of the main heroes featured in *The Transformers: The Movie*. He helps destroy Unicron.

The Movie

In 1986, an animated movie came out. It was *The Transformers: The Movie*. It featured Unicron. Some parents thought the movie was too dark. Fourteen characters die. Megatron kills Optimus Prime.

Unicron

Unicron has several names. He is called Chaos Bringer. He fights as a robot. He can turn into a planet. Then he travels through space. He eats other planets.

Unicron Fail

Hasbro planned a Unicron figure. They built a prototype. But it had weak arm joints. Its sound chip did not work.

Most Unicron figures have horns on the head and wings that come out of the toy's back.

Generation 2

In 1992, Hasbro relaunched Transformers. This was the toy line's first reboot. There were new comics and figures. The line was called Generation 2 (G2).

Many G2 Transformers were updated versions of old characters. G2 Sideswipe, for example, featured different colors than G1 Sideswipe.

New Cartoon

The cartoon rebooted in 1992. It was called *The Transformers: Generation 2.* It featured reruns of G1 episodes. But each had a computer-generated introduction.

Transformers with new features were made as part of the G2 reboot. Laser Rod figures, such as Electro, came with swords that lit up.

The G2 Breakdown figure was released at a convention in 1994.

G2 Figures

G2 toys had new colors. They had spring-loaded weapons. Some had lights. Others made sounds. With these features, the toys looked different. They did not look like the cartoon characters.

Megatron

The G2 Megatron no longer turned into a gun. He changed into an army tank. He was green and purple. He had a camouflage pattern.

The G2 Megatron figure could play several sound effects, including a laser sound and a battle cry.

G2 Comics

Marvel published 12 Transformers comics. They came out between 1993 and 1994. They continued the G1 story. In the comics, Autobots find new Cybertronians. These comics are more violent than earlier ones.

BotCon

In 1994, fans established a Transformers convention. They called it BotCon. It has been held in 18 cities and three countries.

Coloring and activity books based on G2 Transformers storylines came out in the 1990s.

Japanese Comics

Japanese readers had different comics. In these

comics, Megatron and Optimus Prime work together. But humans kill Megatron's friend. Megatron gets mad at the humans. The G2 battles begin.

The G2 comics featured the character Jhiaxus, who was part of the new group of Cybertronians. Several Jhiaxus toys were made in the 2000s.

Transformers Reimagined

In 1996, there was another reboot. It was *Beast Wars: Transformers*. In this series, robots became animals. The robots crash-landed on a planet. It had a big Energon supply. This energy would be bad for their circuits. So the robots turned into animals.

The creators of *Beast Wars: Transformers* used the latest technology to animate the characters' movements and faces.

Many Optimus Primal figures have been made over the years. Most feature black and gray colors.

The Cartoon

Beast Wars: Transformers was set in a jungle. The series had computer-generated animation. It looked three-dimensional. In the show, Autobots were Maximals. Decepticons were Predacons.

Optimus Primal

Optimus Primal is descended from Optimus Prime. On Cybertron, he was a jet. In Beast Wars, he is a gorilla. This form protects him.

FUN FACT!

Beast Wars was the first Transformers show to win an Emmy Award. It won a 1998 Daytime Emmy for animation.

New Features

Beast Wars figures were spring powered. The toys had ball-and-socket joints. If an arm popped out, it could snap back into place. Weapons were stored on the figure.

Waspinator

Waspinator is a Predacon. He is often blown up in battle. Then he must be put back together. But Waspinator never

The first Waspinator figure was released in 1996. It could transform into a green wasp.

gives up. He is determined to win. One Waspinator figure has a stinger gun.

FUN FACT!

Waspinator won the Fans Choice Award at BotCon 2011 in Pasadena, California.

Blackarachnia

Blackarachnia turns into a black widow spider. She arrived on Earth as a Maximal. Predacons captured her. But Blackarachnia is sly. She tricks the Predacons. Then she rejoins the Maximals.

Many Blackarachnia figures were purple and came with a grappling hook weapon.

The 1996 Cheetor figure was yellow with dark spots. In robot form, his hind section and tail turned into a rifle.

Transmetals

During the Beast Wars, Transformers are bathed in a quantum surge. This changes their robotic modes. It gives them organic parts. This means they become beasts with vehicle parts. They are called Transmetals. In 1998, Hasbro launched Beast Wars Transmetal figures.

Cheetor

Cheetor is the fastest Maximal. Fans could buy a Beast Wars Cheetor. They could also buy a

Transmetal Beast Cheetor. This character tries to prove himself. He looks up to Optimus Primal. He calls him "Big Bot."

Iguanus

Iguanus is a Predacon. He comes as a Beast. He also comes as a Transmetal Beast. Iguanus is a strong enemy. He finds enemies from far away. He fires long-range missiles.

The Beast Wars toy line included more than just action figures. One 1997 toy was the Picture View Camera Key Chain.

In Beast Wars, Maximals and Predacons have special symbols. The Maximal symbol has pointed ears.

Beast Wars: Transformers

Beast Wars: Transformers is a video game. It came out in 1997. It was for PlayStation and personal computers (PCs). In the game, Maximals and Predacons fight. They want to control Energon. Players choose a character. They can switch between machine and beast forms.

Beast Wars: Transmetals

Another game came out in 1999. It was *Beast Wars: Transmetals*. This PlayStation game had different endings. One was for Maximals. Another was for Predacons. There was also a Nintendo 64 version of the game. It had more endings.

In the *Beast Wars: Transmetals* game, players engage in one-on-one combat. They can choose to play as a Predacon or Maximal.

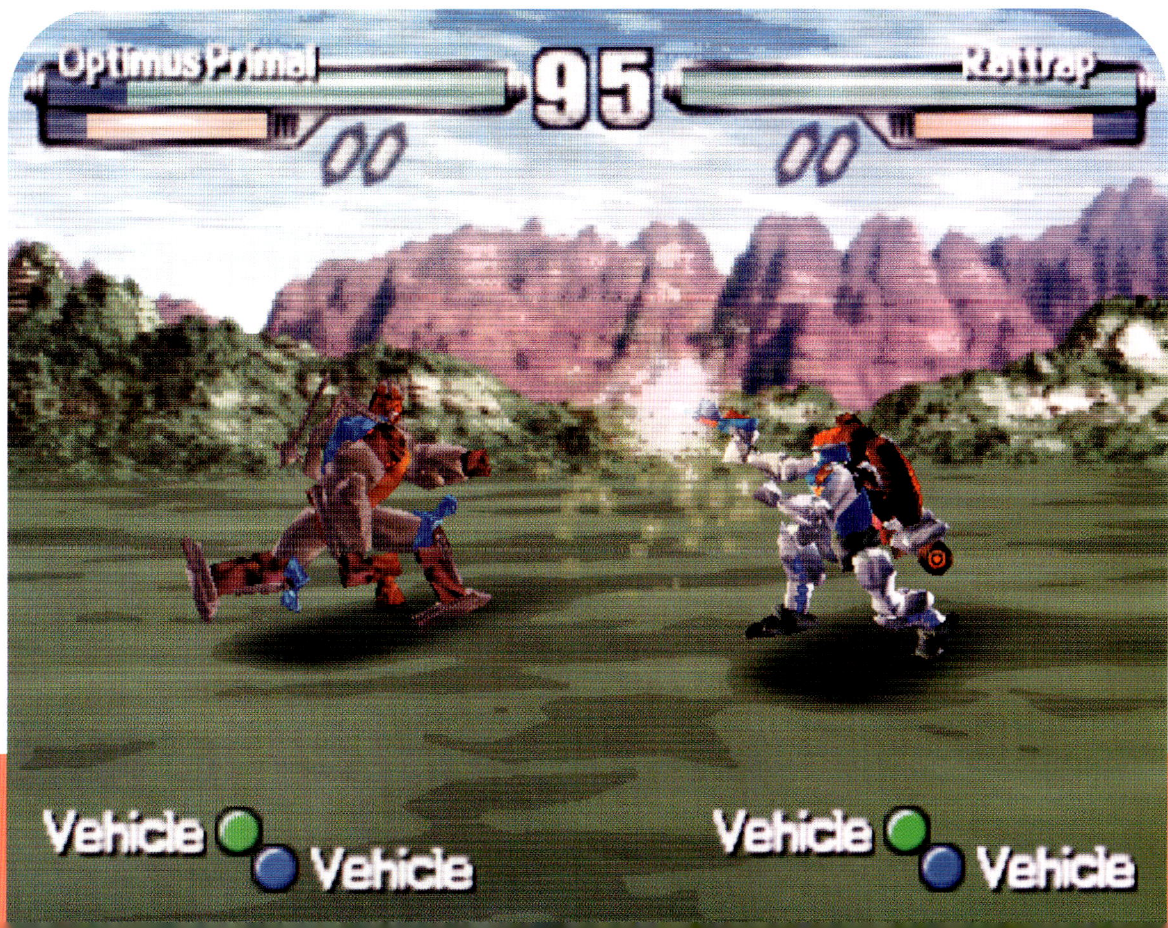

Beast Machines

Beast Machines came out in 1999. The show features Maximals. They fight Vehicons. These are military vehicles. Maximal figures have bright colors. They have translucent plastic.

FUN FACT!

Except for flashbacks, the *Beast Machines* series takes place entirely on Cybertron.

Buzzsaw

Buzzsaw turns into a wasp. He has wings. In robot form, these wings become legs. His left arm is a stinger. The stinger is on a spring.

One Beast Machines figure was Geckobot. This Maximal turned into a winged lizard.

Che is shaped like a cheetah's head. Other Transformer figures can ride on the vehicle's back.

Che

Che is an interceptor craft. It is cheetah inspired. It is fast. It is easy to steer. Cheetor often drives Che. But other Maximals sometimes drive it.

The deluxe version of the Dinobot Triceradon has a mode that makes the toy look like it's playing dead.

Dinobots

Beast Machines were popular. Hasbro wanted to make more figures. It borrowed molds from Japan. They were molds of dinosaur characters. These were from a Japanese series.

Different Sizes

Beast Machines figures have different sizes than the cartoon characters. They are also different colors. The toy designers and animators didn't work together on designs.

Airraptor

Airraptor is a Maximal. He is based on the archaeopteryx. This is a bird-like dinosaur. Airraptor is a good spy. He is fast. But he has fragile wings. They can be hurt by enemy fire.

Dinotron

Dinotron is based on the pachycephalosaurus. This dinosaur has a hard head. In robot form, his head is chest armor. His tail is a sword. The robot has a helmet too.

One Dinobot was called T-Wrecks. It came with a water-squirter weapon and a large claw hand.

Robots in Disguise

Takara wanted to return to the G1 style. It created Transformers: Robots in Disguise (RID). This line launched in 2000. It came out in Japan. In 2001, the figures were released in the United States. RID includes two villain groups. These are Predacons and Decepticons.

The Robots in Disguise line was called Car Robots in Japan. One early Car Robots toy was Art Fire, who was released as Hot Shot in the United States.

Ultra Magnus was featured in several RID cartoons and comics. Some early versions of the character were white and blue.

Anime Series

An RID anime series was made in Japan. It came out in 2000. The show features Megatron and the Predacons. They target Earth. The Autobots hide among humans. They turn into vehicles.

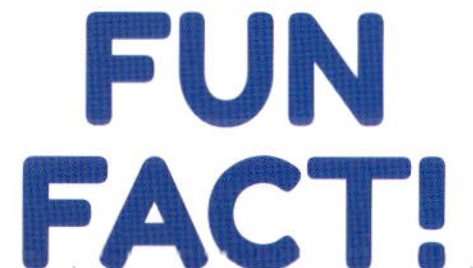

The Japanese name for the US RID cartoon was *Transformers Adventure.*

RID Figures

The RID toy line included new and old characters. Existing molds were used for old characters. But the figures had updated colors. The new characters used new molds. These were detailed.

Optimus Prime

The RID toy line was popular. One figure was Optimus Prime. It turned into a fire truck. Optimus Prime sees the good in others. He lets enemies change sides.

The RID Optimus Prime is sometimes called Fire Convoy. Many toys of this character have been made.

The RID Megatron figure featured purple, black, and orange colors. It had large bat-like wings.

Megatron

RID Megatron has six forms. It can become a robot or a jet. It can be a race car. It can also turn into a dragon. The dragon has two heads. Other forms are a gargoyle and giant hand.

X-Brawn

Three RID Autobots are brothers. X-Brawn is the oldest. He is tough and daring. He loves the outdoors. He drives off road. He can drive underwater too.

In Takara's Car Robots line, X-Brawn was originally called Super Wildride.

Prowl

Prowl is the middle brother. He is a police officer. He turns into a police car. Prowl does everything by the rules. He keeps others out of trouble.

Side Burn

Side Burn is the youngest brother. When given a dull job, his mind wanders. He changes into a blue sports car.

Prowl was one of the original G1 figures. In vehicle form, the G1 toy had the words "Highway Patrol Police" printed on it.

Several Transformers video games were created for PlayStation 2. This gaming console was released in 2000.

The Transformers

In 2003, *The Transformers* came out. It was a PlayStation 2 game. It was released in Japan. In the game, Decepticons and Autobots time travel. They must find the Zel Quartz. This is a power source. When players win missions, they unlock characters.

Dreamwave Comics

Dreamwave is a publisher. It created more Transformers comics. These came out in the early 2000s. One series was *Prime Directive*. In it, Decepticons want to turn Earth into Cybertron. Another series was *War and Peace*. It features Shockwave.

Many Transformers video games and comics came out in the early 2000s. One PlayStation 2 game was called *The Best of Takara: Transformers*.

Armada

The next reboot was *Transformers: Armada*. It was a cartoon. Hasbro and Takara made it. It was released from 2002 to 2003. In the show, Autobots and Decepticons fight. They want to control Mini-Cons. These small Transformers provide power.

Armada Figures

Armada figures were designed to scale. They were larger than earlier figures. Earlier figures were posable. They held weapons. Armada figures had ports. Kids put Mini-Cons into these.

In the early 2000s, several *Transformers: Armada* episodes were released on DVD.

An Armada figure of Scavenger came with a Mini-Con named Rollbar. When Mini-Cons attached to a Transformer, it was called Powerlinxing.

Some Mini-Cons, such as the Land Military Mini-Con Team, were sold in three-packs.

Mini-Cons

Mini-Cons were small Transformers. They added to a Transformer's power. Mini-Cons were like keys. They were inserted into a Transformer's port. Then they unlocked features. These might be sounds. They might be weapons. Mini-Cons came with each figure.

Unicron

One Armada figure was Unicron. It had red eyes. One fist lit up. Unicron was a large figure. It stood 16 inches (41 cm) tall. The toy was popular.

Electronic Features

Larger Armada Transformers figures included electronics. Some featured lights. Others had sound chips. An Armada Optimus Prime figure came with a remote control. It made Optimus Prime's trailer transform.

One Mini-Con was called Sureshock. She could turn into a motor scooter.

Some figures in the Energon and Cybertron toy lines were updated versions of Armada figures. Others, such as Cruellock, were new.

Dead End

Unicron had a Mini-Con. This Mini-Con was named Dead End. It fit into a port in Unicron's chest. This unlocked three missiles.

Unicron Trilogy

Armada inspired two toy lines. It also inspired two cartoons. These were

Energon (2004) and *Cybertron* (2005). These series were part of the Unicron Trilogy. So was Armada.

Beast Wars

Soon, fans wanted more figures. Hasbro added Mini-Con ports to its Beast Wars Transmetal figures. These ports did not unlock features. They were decorative.

Multiple versions of Transformers characters, such as Metroplex, were created for the Unicron Trilogy toy lines. These inspired later figures of the character.

ibooks

In the early 2000s, Transformers books came out. The ibooks company published them. Three were about Keepers. These are aliens. *Transformers: Hardwired* came out in 2003. In this story, Keepers make Transformers fight. *Transformers: Fusion* came out in 2004. In this book, Transformers fight Keepers. They fight the US military too.

Board games and card games based on the Unicron Trilogy came out in the 2000s. One was called Transformers Armada: Battle for Cybertron.

G.I. Joe

Crossover comics were also published. One was *G.I. Joe vs. The Transformers*. It came out in 2003. This comic features an evil group called Cobra. It finds dormant Transformers. *Transformers/G.I. Joe* came out in 2004. It is set during World War II (1939–1945).

Many G.I. Joe toys were action figures inspired by branches of the US military, such as the US Marine Corps.

Energon figures were released in waves, such as the Energon Class, Combat Class, and Command Class. The Energon Class included characters such as Doom-Lock.

Energon

In 2004, *Transformers: Energon* aired. This cartoon had 51 episodes. It takes place ten years after *Armada*. Autobots and Decepticons are at peace. They mine Energon together. Then Alpha Q arrives. He wants to work with Megatron and Unicron. He plans to restart the war.

Animation

The *Energon* series had hand-drawn animation. It also had computer-generated animation. Most robots were computer generated. Some fans didn't like this. They said the robots looked stiff.

Demolishor was one Decepticon featured in the *Energon* cartoon. Several figures of the character were made.

The Energon toy line featured several Optimus Prime figures. One came with mini vehicles that combined to form a larger figure.

Energon Figures

Energon figures came with weapons. These were made of translucent plastic. The figures could combine. They created larger robots. These were called Combiner sets. One robot was the body. Four others were the limbs.

Role-Playing

Some Energon toys were weapons. They were human-size. With these, fans could join the fight between good and evil. They could swing Energon swords. They could fire Energon blasters.

The Optimus Prime Energon Blaster toy came with foam Nerf darts.

Cybertron

Transformers: Cybertron launched in 2005. In this cartoon, there is a black hole. It threatens the universe. Autobots must stop it. They must find four Cyber Planet Keys. They must find them before Megatron does.

The Cybertron line included several sublines, including one called Legends of Cybertron. These small figures involved simple transformations.

Cyber Planet Keys were shaped like discs. Each key featured a design based on a Transformer's home planet.

Cyber Planet Key

Cybertron figures came with Cyber Planet Keys. These unlocked features on the figure. Sometimes these were weapons. The key also had a code. Fans could use it on the Transformers website. It unlocked photos and facts.

Cyber Planets

In *Cybertron*, there are six planets. Each has its own key and vehicles. Earth Planet has jets and cars. Jungle Planet has mechanical beasts. Unicron's followers come from Planet X.

Skywarp

Skywarp is an Earth Planet Transformer. He turns into a jet. He can teleport. This power is called warping. It carries him from place to place.

Skywarp is known for being a prankster and is the only Decepticon who can teleport.

Snarl

Snarl is from the Jungle Planet. He turns into a wolf. He carries a missile launcher. His wolf tail shoots missiles. He is unlike other Jungle Planet Transformers. This is because he has long-distance weapons.

In the *Cybertron* cartoon, Scourge is the leader of the Jungle Planet. He turns into a dragon.

The Gathering

In 2006, IDW published *Beast Wars: The Gathering*. This was a comic series. It continued the *Transformers: Beast Wars* story. In the books, Autobots fight Magmatron. He is a Predacon.

The Ascending

In October 2007, another comic series launched. It was *Beast Wars: The Ascending*. This story features Shokaract. He is a Predacon warlord. He wants to be a god. He feeds on Unicron's life force.

Some Shokaract figures turn into a large crab. Others transform into a hovercraft.

IDW has published many Transformers comics and books. In 2022, it released the comic book *Declaration of War*.

Transformers Movie

In 2007, the first live-action Transformers movie came out. It features teen Sam Witwicky. Sam buys a car. It turns into Bumblebee. Soon Sam is in the middle of a Transformers war. Fans liked the movie's action. They liked its effects.

Peter Cullen

Peter Cullen is a voice actor. He voiced Optimus Prime in *The Transformers* cartoon. He voiced the character in the 1986 and 2007 movies too.

Actor Shia LaBeouf played Sam Witwicky in the 2007 *Transformers* film.

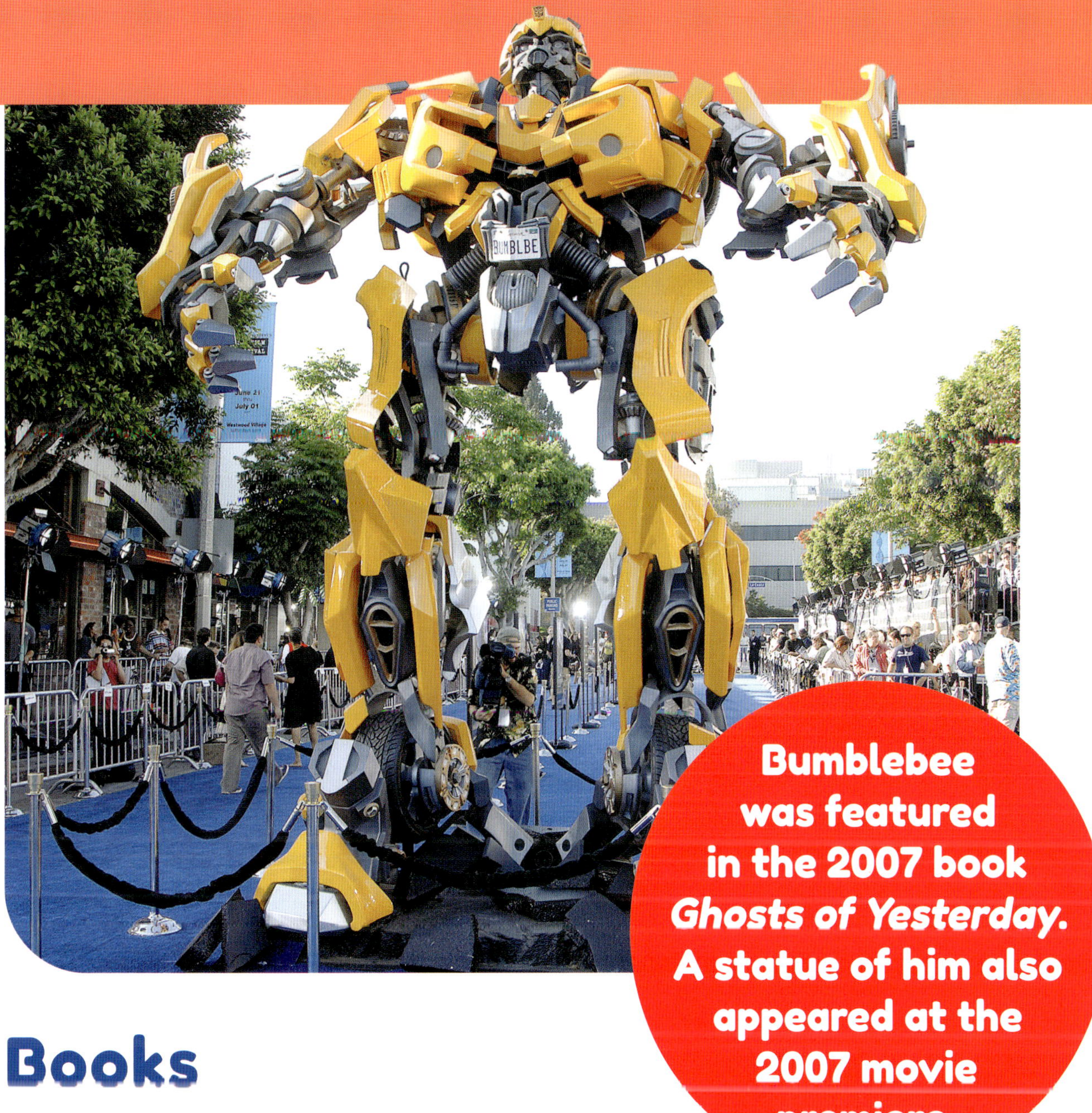

Bumblebee was featured in the 2007 book *Ghosts of Yesterday*. A statue of him also appeared at the 2007 movie premiere.

Books

Transformers books were also released. Many were for adults. Alan Dean Foster wrote two of them. One was *Transformers: Ghosts of Yesterday*. It came out in 2007. It features a Transformer found in ice.

TRANSFORMERS (2007)

Transformers: The Game **included multiple levels and bonus content. Gamers could play as popular characters such as Bumblebee.**

Video Game

In 2007, *Transformers: The Game* was released. It was based on the 2007 movie. It was for PCs. The game was also for consoles. Gamers could play as Autobots. Or they could be Decepticons.

Nintendo DS Games

In 2007, two more games came out. They were for Nintendo DS. *Transformers Autobots* focuses on Autobots. Another was *Transformers Decepticons.* It is about Decepticons. Each game has missions. Gamers can create their own robot.

The Nintendo DS was first released in 2004. The company Activision developed the 2007 Transformers games for the console.

Animated

In 2007, Cartoon Network released *Transformers: Animated*. In the United States, this series ran until 2009. In the show, Transformers crash on Earth. After 50 years, they wake up. They must find the AllSpark. This can create new Transformers.

Transformers: Animated **figures were designed to closely resemble the cartoon characters. Many figures had softer features and rounded edges.**

The *Transformers: Animated* Bulkhead figure features claw hands and a wrecking ball weapon. It can turn into a military van.

Bulkhead

Bulkhead is in *Transformers: Animated*. He is Bumblebee's best friend. He wants to be an artist. He is a careful fighter. He doesn't want to hurt anyone weaker than himself.

Lockdown features black and green colors and has a hook on his hand. The figure transforms into a sports car.

Lockdown

Lockdown is a bounty hunter. He first appeared in *Transformers: Animated*. He isn't an Autobot. He isn't a Decepticon either. But he often works for Decepticons. This is because they pay better. He keeps Transformer parts as trophies.

Lugnut

Lugnut is gigantic. Unlike other Decepticons, he is loyal. He does his best to serve Megatron. He likes destroying things.

The *Transformers: Animated* Lugnut figure comes with a large mace. The figure turns into a bomber plane.

Revenge of the Fallen

Another live-action movie came out in 2009. It was *Revenge of the Fallen*. In the movie, Sam Witwicky is in college. He starts seeing symbols. They are clues to a machine. It is in Egypt. The Decepticons want to use it. They plan to destroy Earth's sun.

Many ads for *Transformers: Revenge of the Fallen* featured the pyramids of Egypt. In the film, a battle takes place near the pyramids.

The character Devastator is featured in *Revenge of the Fallen*. Six Constructicons combine to create this huge Transformer.

Books

The movie led to more books. One was *Transformers: The Veiled Threat* (2009). Alan Dean Foster wrote it. In this story, humans and Autobots work together. Another book was *Transformers: Exodus* (2010). It is about Optimus Prime and Megatron. It explains how they became enemies.

Prime

Transformers: Prime started in 2010. This cartoon had three seasons. In the show, three teens join the Autobots. Megatron returns from space. He brings Dark Energon. It turns Transformers into zombies. Megatron builds a zombie army.

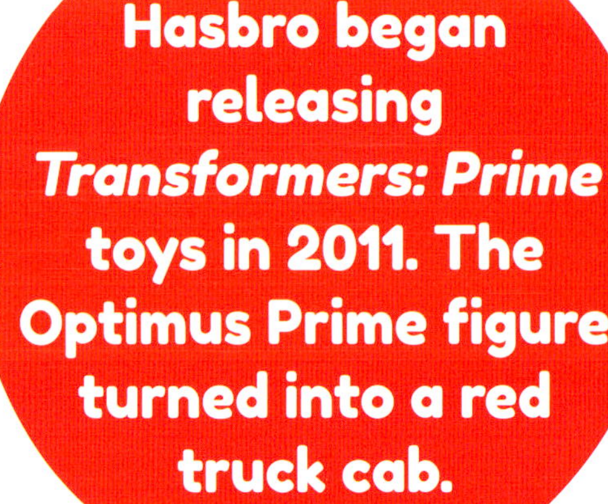
Hasbro began releasing *Transformers: Prime* toys in 2011. The Optimus Prime figure turned into a red truck cab.

Knock Out

Knock Out is a Decepticon who is a doctor. Most Decepticons change into aircraft. But Knock Out changes into a sports car. He is proud and one of a kind.

FUN FACT!

For *Transformers: Prime*, character designers changed Arcee from pink and white to blue.

Arcade Games

In 2010, two arcade games came out. They were released in Japan. One was *Transformers Animated: The Chase*. The other was *Transformers Animated: The Shooting*. *Transformers: Prime* figures came with cards. Players inserted a character's card into the games. Then they could play as that character.

Many Transformers arcade games have been released. Several were designed by video game company Sega.

Console Games

Console games were also released. *War for Cybertron* came out in 2010. It takes place during a Cybertron war. Megatron seeks Dark Energon. He wants to use it to change the planet. Many fans liked the voice acting. They also liked the multiplayer options.

The *War for Cybertron* game shared a name with a toy line called the War for Cybertron Trilogy.

Dark of the Moon

In 2011, another live-action movie came out. It was *Transformers: Dark of the Moon*. In the movie, astronauts find a spacecraft. It is on the moon. The craft is from Cybertron. The film featured Shockwave.

Michael Bay directed several Transformers movies, including *Dark of the Moon*. In 2011, he attended a screening of the film in London, England.

Transformers: Dark of the Moon starred Shia LaBeouf as Sam and Rosie Huntington-Whiteley as Sam's girlfriend, Carly.

Sentinel Prime

Dark of the Moon featured Sentinel Prime. He once led the Autobots. He turns into an airport fire truck. In the film, he works with Megatron. He plans to sacrifice Earth to fix Cybertron.

In the *Dark of the Moon* video game, gamers could play as Autobots or Decepticons. One featured Decepticon was Megatron.

Games

A *Dark of the Moon* video game came out in 2011. Gamers play as robots. Or they can be vehicles. This was a new feature. It was called Stealth Force. The vehicles are armed. They can take damage.

Books

Novels based on *Dark of the Moon* also came out. *Transformers: Exiles* was published in 2011. In the book, Optimus Prime destroys Cybertron. He wants to stop Megatron.

Optimus Prime was frequently featured in *Dark of the Moon* merchandise. Some figures of the character had detailed armor and large cannons.

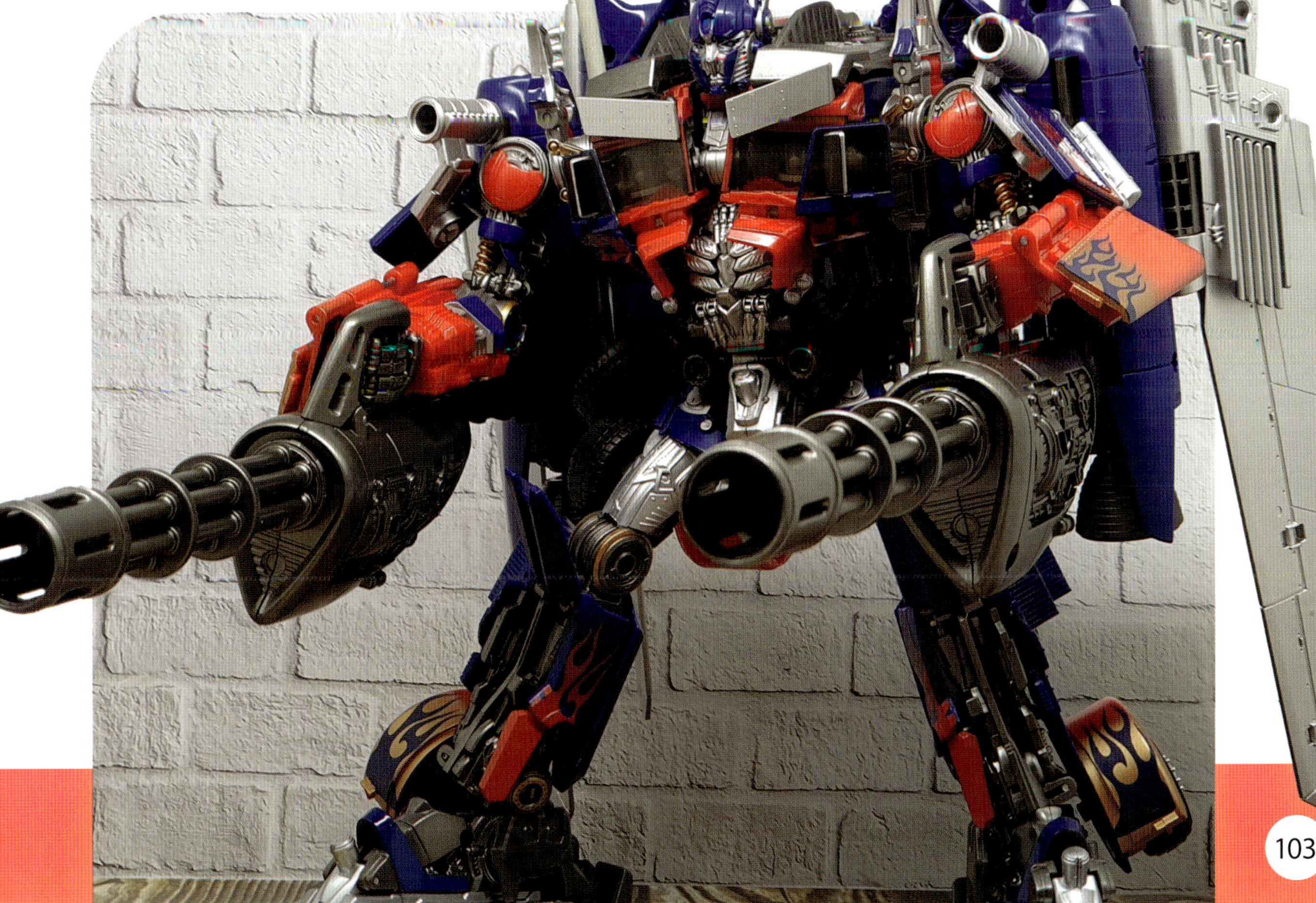

Fall of Cybertron

In 2012, *Transformers: Fall of Cybertron* was released. This was a fighting game. It was for PCs. It was also for consoles. In the game, Autobots build a ship. They plan to leave Cybertron. But Decepticons attack.

In 2012, *Transformers: Fall of Cybertron* was featured at a gaming conference in Los Angeles, California.

Rise of the Dark Spark

In 2014, *Transformers: Rise of the Dark Spark* came out. It was for PCs and consoles. In the game, Autobots and Decepticons try to control the Dark Spark. This is a treasure. It controls the universe. Some fans said the game's design felt rushed.

Covenant of Primus

Transformers: The Covenant of Primus is a book. It came out in 2013. Justina Robson wrote it. It came in a case. The case had an Autobot emblem. When opened, sound effects played. Readers learn the history of Transformers.

Justina Robson has written many science fiction books.

Windblade

In 2014, Hasbro introduced Windblade. She appeared in *Dark Cybertron*. This is a comic. Windblade turns into a jet. She takes off and lands vertically.

Windblade is usually red with blue details. Her wings have rotating fans on them.

Age of Extinction

In 2014, *Transformers: Age of Extinction* came out. It is a live-action film. In the film, Earth has been saved. A human bounty hunter looks for Transformers. A mechanic buys Optimus Prime. He helps him.

Transformers: Age of Extinction **features the Dinobots. Ads for the film showed Optimus Prime riding on the back of a T. rex.**

Most Drift figures are blue and feature a samurai-inspired design.

Drift

Drift was once a Decepticon. He was Deadlock. He is left behind after a battle. Other Transformers find him. They fix him. Then he becomes Drift. He uses swords.

Alternate Modes

Originally, Drift's alternate mode was a Nissan Silvia S15. But then his form changed. He changed to a Bugatti Veyron or a helicopter. He has three forms.

TRANSFORMERS: AGE OF EXTINCTION

A statue of Crosshairs, *left*, appeared near a site in Chongqing, China. Scenes from *Age of Extinction* were filmed there.

Crosshairs

Crosshairs appears in *Age of Extinction*. He is tired of war. He does not want to fight. He changes into a Corvette. In robot form, the car's body panels fit like a coat.

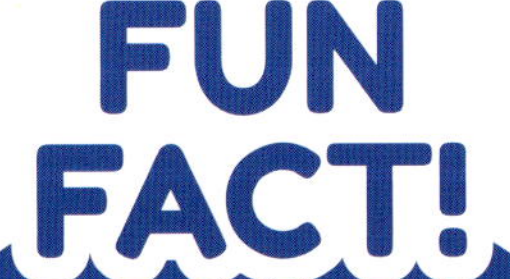

In *Transformers: Age of Extinction*, Hound and Crosshairs never transform on-screen.

Hound

Hound is a small Autobot. His size makes him a good scout. He carries a hologram gun. It collects images. Hound can display the images as holograms.

The *Age of Extinction* version of Hound is army green and has a beard.

TRANSFORMERS: THE LAST KNIGHT

A poster for *The Last Knight* featured Optimus Prime holding a sword. The film's story is based on the legend of King Arthur and his knights.

The Last Knight

Transformers: The Last Knight came out in 2017. It is a live-action film. In it, Optimus Prime returns to Cybertron. He learns how to restore the planet. He must find an artifact on Earth. This will help him steal Earth's energy core.

IMAX

Michael Bay filmed *Transformers: The Last Knight* for IMAX theaters. The film was shot with two cameras. One sat atop the other. This provides detail and depth.

Canopy

Canopy appears in *The Last Knight*. He wears a debris shell. This lets him hide among city ruins. Canopy shelters Izabella and Sqweeks. Izabella is a human orphan. Sqweeks is a small robot. Canopy hides them from Decepticons.

Actress Isabela Merced played the orphan Izabella in *The Last Knight*.

Cogman

The Last Knight features Cogman. He is a small Transformer. He is a butler. He works for the Burton family. They are Witwiccans. This is a group of humans. They have long known about Transformers.

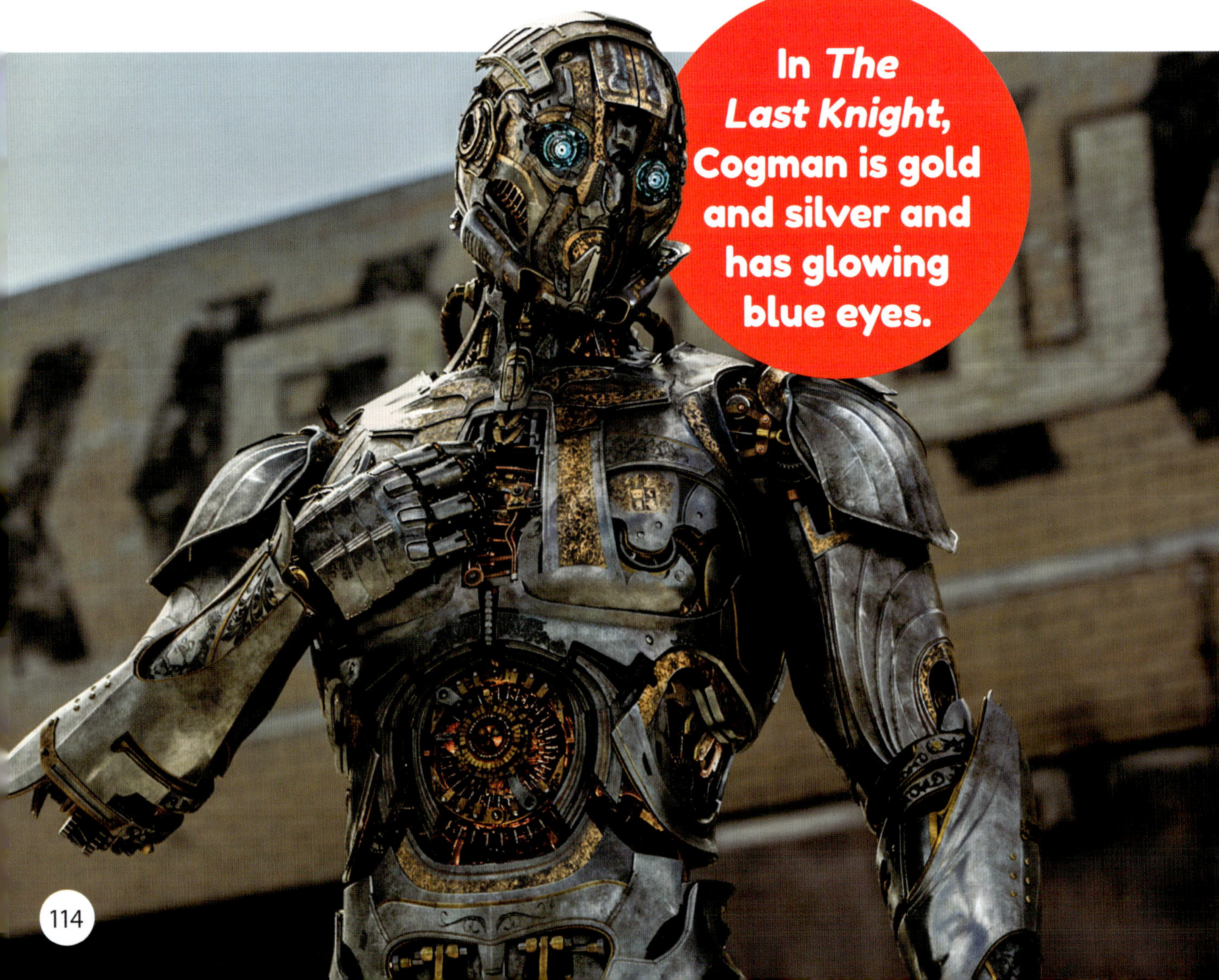

In *The Last Knight*, Cogman is gold and silver and has glowing blue eyes.

Nemesis Prime

In *The Last Knight*, Optimus Prime meets Quintessa. She is a Cybertron goddess. She brainwashes Optimus Prime. He turns evil. He becomes Nemesis Prime.

FUN FACT!

Cogman is a Headmaster, a Transformer that becomes a larger robot's head.

In *The Last Knight*, Optimus Prime has armor-like plates and a shield. When he becomes Nemesis Prime, his eyes turn purple.

Bumblebee

A live-action movie came out in 2018. It was *Transformers: Bumblebee*. It takes place in 1987.

Bumblebee hides in a junkyard. He is in vehicle form. Teen Charlie takes the car home. She learns it is a Transformer.

Transformers: Bumblebee **starred Hailee Steinfeld as Charlie and John Cena as Agent Jack Burns.**

An Adventure

In the movie, Bumblebee has lost his voice in battle. His memory is damaged too. Charlie becomes friends with Bumblebee. They work together to fix Bumblebee's memory. They also help defeat Decepticons on Earth.

Bumblebee Model

The *Bumblebee* crew built a Bumblebee model. It was life size. It even had eyes that lit up.

Many exclusive action figures were modeled after the movie version of Bumblebee.

Cyberverse

Transformers: Cyberverse is a cartoon. It ran from 2018 to 2021. In the series, Bumblebee's memory is damaged. Windblade helps him recover the data. The series has computer animation. It looks like a comic book.

The *Cyberverse* Clobber figure is purple and can transform into a hovercraft.

Megatron X

In *Transformers: Cyberverse,* Megatron is Megatron X. He is an enemy. He wants to destroy Optimus Prime. Megatron X is crueler than Megatron. He turns into a tank.

In *Transformers: Cyberverse,* Megatron X has a black color scheme. Many toy versions of Megatron also have darker colors.

Rise of the Beasts

Transformers: Rise of the Beasts came out in 2023. It is a live-action film. In the movie, Unicron eats the Maximals' home world. The Maximals join the Autobots. They defend Earth. They fight Terrorcons. These look like reptiles.

Rise of the Beasts **was based on Hasbro's Beast Wars toy line. It featured fan-favorite characters such as Optimus Prime and Arcee.**

Scourge

Scourge leads the Terrorcons. He is a trophy hunter. He turns into a logging truck. Scourge uses Unicron's dark energy. He uses it to make Maximals evil.

Scourge is the main villain in *Rise of the Beasts*. The Titan Changer Scourge figure could transform into a truck in just four steps.

Airazor was featured in a *Rise of the Beasts* toy line called Beast Battle Masters. The small bird figure transforms into a crossbow blaster.

Airazor

Airazor appears in *Rise of the Beasts*. She is a Maximal. Her beast mode is a falcon. She has feathers. In the movie, Scourge turns Airazor evil.

FUN FACT!

Oscar-winning actress Michelle Yeoh voices Airazor.

Optimus Primal

In *Rise of the Beasts,* Optimus Prime is Optimus Primal. He changes into a jet. His animal form is a gorilla. He uses rockets to fly. In gorilla form, Optimus Primal has swords.

In 2023, a large statue of Optimus Primal was displayed in London's Leicester Square to celebrate the premiere of *Rise of the Beasts.*

New Comics

Image Comics rebooted Transformers comics in 2024. The *Transformers* series features Autobots and Decepticons. They are on a new planet. They don't know what happened to Cybertron. Daniel Warren Johnson wrote the comics.

Transformers One

Transformers One came out in 2024. It is animated. In the film, Optimus Prime is Orion Pax.

Actor Chris Hemsworth voices Orion Pax in *Transformers One*. He attended the film's premiere in London, England.

Transformers Movies

Transformers movies have generated a lot of money over the years. The films have helped make Transformers into a successful franchise.

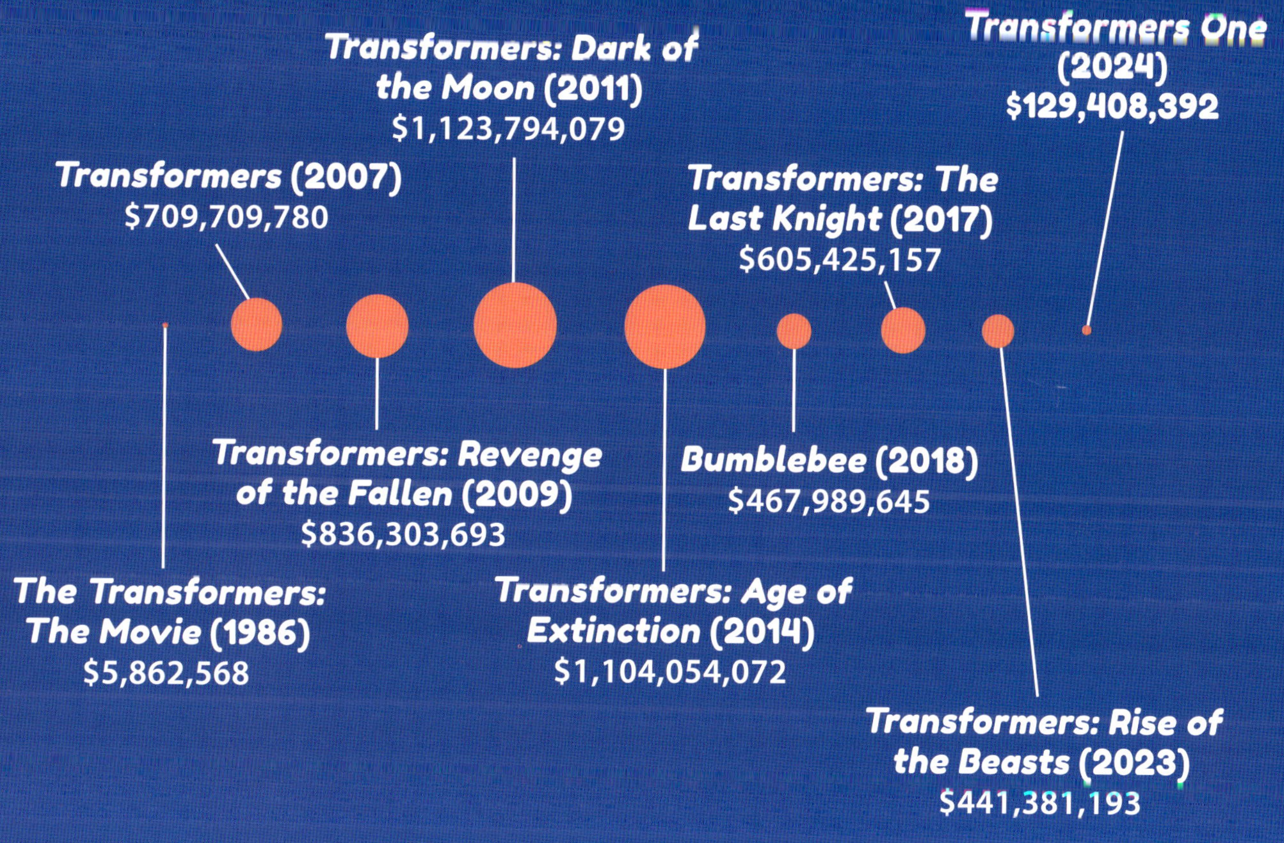

Megatron is D-16. They are friends. They are low-ranking workers. To transform, they must visit Cybertron's surface.

GLOSSARY

asset
Something useful or valuable.

camouflage
A color pattern that is used to hide things or make them blend in.

cassette
A sealed plastic case that contains audio tape for recording sound.

descend
To be related to a person or group that lived in the past.

dormant
Asleep or not active.

gargoyle
A decorative water spout shaped like a scary human or animal figure on a building's roof.

interceptor
Something that stops or catches something or someone.

medic
Someone trained to treat injuries.

minion
An underling or follower.

mold
A hollow container used to make a consistent shape.

organic
Of or relating to living things.

prototype
The first version or model of something.

radiation
A type of energy in the form of waves or particles.

reboot
A new or updated version of a franchise, such as a toy line.

scout
To sneak into an area to spy.

translucent
Semitransparent. Not clear but allowing light to pass through.

TO LEARN MORE

More Books to Read

Buckey, A. W. *Hot Wheels*. Abdo, 2026.

Gale, Ryan. *Lego*. Abdo, 2026.

Snider, Brandon T. *What Is the Story of Transformers?* Penguin Workshop, 2022.

Online Resources

To learn more about Transformers, please visit **abdobooklinks.com** or scan this QR code. These links are routinely monitored and updated to provide the most current information available.

INDEX

PHOTO CREDITS

Cover Photos: Chris Willson/Alamy, front (Optimus Prime); iStockphoto, front (Bumblebee); Adobe Stock, front (Bumblebee in box), back; Shutterstock Images, front (truck)

Interior Photos: iStockphoto, 1, 19, 90; Fabinho Silva/Shutterstock Images, 3; Shutterstock Images, 4, 6 (bottom), 12, 13, 15 (top), 18, 27, 30, 32 (top), 33, 35, 41 (top), 46 (top), 49, 54, 58 (bottom), 61, 62, 66, 71 (top), 72 (bottom), 79, 86 (bottom), 91, 95, 98, 102, 103, 109 (left), 109 (right), 110, 111, 112 (bottom), 115, 117 (top), 117 (bottom), 119, 120; Universal History Archive/Universal Images Group/Getty Images, 5; The Micronauts Wiki, 6 (top); www.benstoybarn.com/Alamy, 7, 32 (bottom); Courtesy of The Strong National Museum of Play, Rochester, New York, USA, 8, 20, 26, 39, 44, 46 (bottom), 53, 56, 65, 67, 68, 73, 74, 76, 78; Chris Willson/Alamy, 9, 17; Imaginechina Limited/Alamy, 10; BFA/DEG/Alamy, 11; Transformers Wiki, 14, 23, 24, 28, 29, 34, 38, 42, 43, 45, 47, 50, 51, 52, 57, 58 (top), 59, 60, 63, 64, 69, 70, 71 (bottom), 72 (top), 77, 81, 82, 83, 84, 92, 93, 96, 97, 105, 107, 118, 121, 122; Clive Rowley/Alamy, 15 (bottom), 16; Niall Carson/PA Images/Getty Images, 21; Jason DeCrow/Invision for Hasbro/AP Images, 22; Nick Ansell/PA Wire/AP Images, 25; Karen Warren/Houston Chronicle/Hearst Newspapers/Getty Images, 31; ZUMA Press, Inc./Alamy, 36; Museum of Hartlepool, 37; RGR Collection/Alamy, 40, 48; Christy Radecic/Invision/AP Images, 41 (bottom); ArcadeImages/Alamy, 55, 88; Tim Boyle/Getty Images News/Getty Images, 75; Morry Gash/AP Images, 80; Zety Akhzar/Shutterstock Images, 85; Andrii Bezvershenko/Shutterstock Images, 86 (top); Frank Trapper/Corbis Entertainment/Getty Images, 87; Evan Amos/Wikimedia Commons, 89; Gustavo Caballero/Getty Images for Paramount Pictures/Getty Images Entertainment/Getty Images, 94; James McDowall/Shutterstock Images, 99; Ian West/PA Images/Getty Images, 100; BFA/Paramount Pictures/Alamy, 101, 116; Kevork Djansezian/Getty Images News/Getty Images, 104; Jesse Wild/SFX Magazine/Future/Getty Images, 106; Caroline McCredie/Getty Images for Paramount Pictures International/Getty Images Entertainment/Getty Images, 108; Gabe Ginsberg/WireImage/Getty Images, 112 (top); Debby Wong/Shutterstock Images, 113; Paramount Pictures/Entertainment Pictures/Alamy, 114; Kate Green/Getty Images for Paramount Pictures UK/Getty Images Entertainment/Getty Images, 123; Fred Duval/Shutterstock Images, 124; Red Line Editorial, 125